Good Food

I Like Ice Cream
By Robin Pickering

Children's Press
A Division of Grolier Publishing
New York / London / Hong Kong / Sydney
Danbury, Connecticut

Photo Credits: Cover, pp. 5, 9, 11, 13, 15, 17, 19 © Adriana Skura;
p. 7 © Juan Silva/ImageBank; p. 21 © Nelson Sa
Contributing Editor: Jennifer Ceaser
Book Design: Nelson Sa

Visit Children's Press on the Internet at:
http://publishing.grolier.com

Library of Congress Cataloging-in-Publication Data

Pickering, Robin.
  I like ice cream / by Robin Pickering.
    p. cm. — (Good food)
  Includes bibliographical references and index.
  Summary: Briefly describes how ice cream is made and some of the ways in which it can be enjoyed.
  ISBN 0-516-23085-9 (lib. bdg.) — ISBN 0-516-23010-7 (pbk.)
    1. Ice cream, ices, etc.—Juvenile literature. [1. Ice cream, ices, etc.] I. Title.

TX795.P53 2000
641.8′62—dc21

00-024374

Copyright © 2000 by Rosen Book Works, Inc.
All rights reserved. Published simultaneously in Canada.
Printed in the United States of America.
    4 5 6 7 8 9 10 R 05 04 03

Contents

1	I Like Ice Cream	4
2	Strawberry Ice Cream	8
3	Vanilla and Chocolate	12
4	Milk Shake	16
5	New Words	22
6	To Find Out More	23
7	Index	24
8	About the Author	24

I like ice cream on a hot day.

Ice cream is cold.

Ice cream is sweet.

Ice cream is made with sugar and milk.

The sugar and milk are mixed with other **flavors**.

Then the mix is **frozen**.

7

I like strawberry ice cream.

It is pink and full of strawberries!

I like **chocolate chip** ice cream.

It is made with **vanilla** ice cream and chocolate chips.

I like soft ice cream.

I like vanilla and chocolate mixed together.

I like ice cream **sundaes**.

A sundae has chocolate **syrup**.

It has nuts and a cherry on top, too.

15

We like to share a **milk shake**.

A milk shake is very **thick**.

It is made with milk and ice cream.

I like **sprinkles** on my ice cream.

Sprinkles make ice cream more fun to eat!

How do you like to eat ice cream?

New Words

chocolate chip (**chok**-lit **chip**) a small piece of chocolate
flavors (**flay**-verz) certain tastes that foods have
frozen (**froh**-zin) made hard from cold
milk shake (**milk shayk**) a drink made by mixing milk and ice cream together
sprinkles (**spring**-kelz) tiny pieces of candy
sundaes (**sun**-dayz) dishes of ice cream with toppings
syrup (**sir**-ep) a sweet topping poured over ice cream
thick (**thik**) not thin; does not flow fast
vanilla (vuh-**nil**-uh) sweet flavoring from a kind of bean

To Find Out More

Books
From Cow to Ice Cream: A Photo Essay
by Bertram T. Knight
Children's Press

Let's Find Out About Ice Cream
by Mary E. Reid
Scholastic

Web Sites
Ice Cream Alliance Home Page
http://www.ice-cream.org/educ_menu.htm
Check out cool facts about ice cream on this site.

The Ice Cream Scoop
http://www.edys.com/scoop/index.html
This site tells about the history of ice cream and names the top ten flavors.

Index

chocolate chip, 10

flavors, 6
frozen, 6

milk shake, 16

sprinkles, 18
strawberry, 8
sundaes, 14
syrup, 14

thick, 16

vanilla, 10, 12

About the Author

Robin Pickering is a writer, editor, and yoga instructor living in Brooklyn, New York.

Reading Consultants

Kris Flynn, Coordinator, Small School District Literacy, The San Diego County Office of Education

Shelly Forys, Certified Reading Recovery Specialist, W.J. Zahnow Elementary School, Waterloo, IL

Peggy McNamara, Professor, Bank Street College of Education, Reading and Literacy Program